INCLUDES OVER AN HOUR OF VIDEO INSTRUCTION

GUITAR BOOT CAMP

AN ALL-INCLUSIVE GUIDE TO SHAPING YOUR TECHNIQUE

BY JASON BUSSE

To access video visit:
www.halleonard.com/mylibrary

Enter Code
4179-8596-5773-4564

ISBN 978-1-4950-9976-2

HAL•LEONARD®

Visit Hal Leonard Online at
www.halleonard.com

Contact us:
Hal Leonard
7777 West Bluemound Road
Milwaukee, WI 53213
Email: info@halleonard.com

In Europe, contact:
Hal Leonard Europe Limited
42 Wigmore Street
Marylebone, London, W1U 2RN
Email: info@halleonardeurope.com

In Australia, contact:
Hal Leonard Australia Pty. Ltd.
4 Lentara Court
Cheltenham, Victoria, 3192 Australia
Email: info@halleonard.com.au

CONTENTS

SECTION 1: BASIC TRAINING

This section introduces the guitar and covers the most important concepts. You will depend on these fundamentals as you continue to hone your guitar-playing skills, so pay attention and don't skip past the drills.

What we'll learn:

CHAPTER 1: FUNDAMENTALS

Parts of the Guitar, Numbering the Fingers, Holding the Guitar and the Pick, Plucking Strings, Fretting Notes, and Moving Between Strings at the Same Fret

CHAPTER 2: NOTES ON THE GUITAR

Names of the Strings, the Musical Alphabet and Basic Intervals, Naming the Notes on a String, and the Fretboard Roadmap

CHAPTER 3: MUTING

Palm Muting, Muffled Strings, Handling Background Noise, and Raking

CHAPTER 4: STRUMMING

Steady Strumming Motion, Eighth-Note Strumming, 16th-Note Strumming, Syncopation, and Swung Eighth Notes

CHAPTER 1: FUNDAMENTALS

PARTS OF THE GUITAR

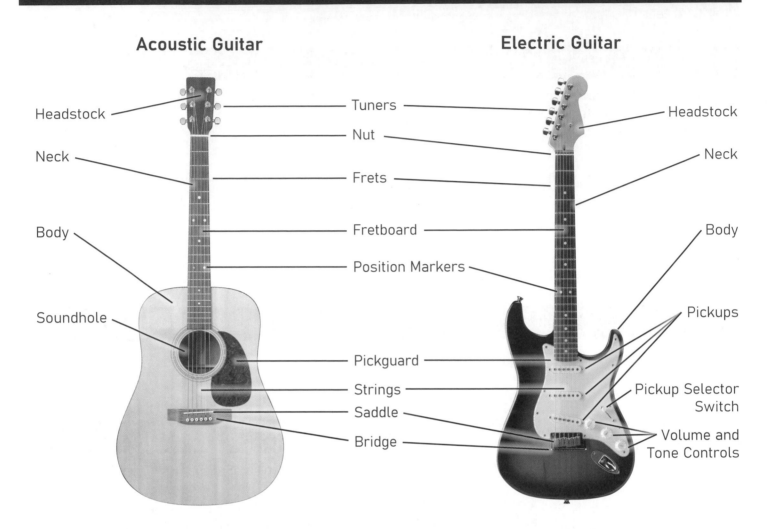

Acoustic Guitar

Electric Guitar

Headstock — Tuners — Headstock

Nut

Neck — Neck

Frets

Body — Fretboard — Body

Soundhole — Position Markers

Pickups

Pickguard

Strings — Pickup Selector Switch

Saddle — Volume and Tone Controls

Bridge

NUMBERING THE FINGERS

When playing the guitar, we call our index finger the first finger, the middle finger is the second, the ring finger is the third, and the pinky is the fourth. The thumb is called, well... the thumb!

HOLDING THE GUITAR AND THE PICK

When seated, the thinnest part of the guitar's body (where it curves inward) should be resting on your leg. Hold the guitar against your body by resting the elbow of your picking hand on the front edge of the body. This should keep the instrument basically positioned straight up and down, with the neck pointing slightly upward. You should be able to strum the strings by moving the elbow of your strumming arm while putting little or no effort into holding the guitar with your fretting hand.

The pick should rest against the side of your index finger. Use the pad of your thumb to hold the pick, allowing just a tiny amount of its tip to show below your grip. You should be able to change the angle of the pick very easily by moving the thumb and index finger. Holding the pick correctly feels similar to the way you hold a pencil against your middle finger. When you pluck or strum the strings, move your strumming arm just like you would if you were striking a nail with a hammer. Start at the elbow and flick your wrist slightly as you move down to make the strings vibrate towards the other strings. Don't rotate your wrist or pull your arm away from the guitar.

FRETTING NOTES

When we pluck an open string, that string is vibrating from the saddle, on the bridge, and the nut. Fretting a note simply means making the string come into contact with one of the frets. This limits the vibrating portion of the string—that is, the section that is between the saddle and the fret that is in front of our finger (towards the bridge). Place your finger as close to the fret as you can without sliding past it. Don't try to squeeze the string down to the fretboard; apply just enough pressure to make it firmly contact the fret.

Exercise 1: Fretting and Speed

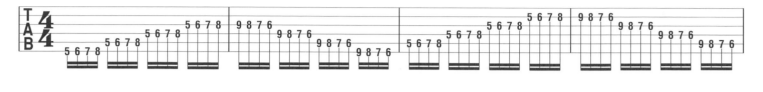

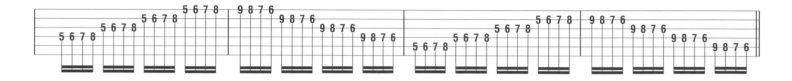

MOVING BETWEEN STRINGS AT THE SAME FRET

When playing notes at the same fret on adjacent strings, we want to use the same finger for both strings, but we also want to avoid a pause or unnecessary noise that can occur as a result of lifting our finger from one string and then placing it down on the next one. There are two useful techniques to help out in these situations: 1) rolling your finger, or 2) barring the strings.

What we mean by rolling your finger is to use the pad of your finger to play the thinner string while using the tip of your finger to play the thicker string. You can slightly change the degree to which your finger is bent to effectively roll the fingertip when switching between strings. We roll when we want to isolate the notes so that only one pitch is allowed to ring at any time.

Barring the strings is when we lay one finger across more than one string. This takes some practice to accomplish and is crucial for playing certain chords. Unlike rolling the finger, this technique allows the strings to continue ringing as we move our pick from one string to the next.

Exercise 2: Rolling

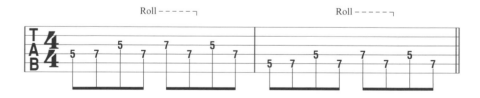

Exercise 3: Rolling

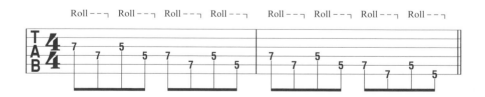

Exercise 4: "Are You Sleeping?"

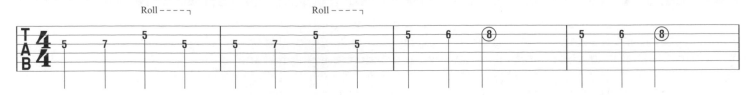

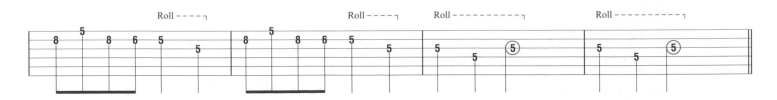

Exercise 5: Barring

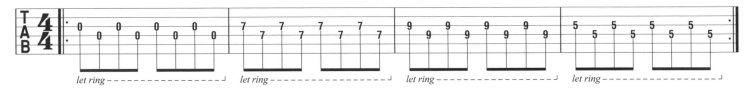

Exercise 6: Barring

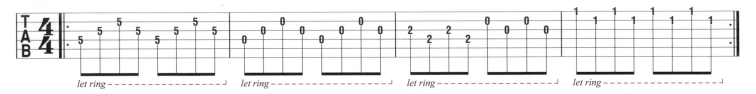

CHAPTER 2: NOTES ON THE GUITAR

NAMES OF THE STRINGS

We number the strings 1 through 6, from highest sounding to lowest sounding. When we name them, we go in the opposite direction, starting at the thickest string and ending at the thinnest. From low to high, the strings are tuned: E–A–D–G–B–E. To help you learn the names of the strings, use this mnemonic device: **E**ddie **A**te **D**ynamite **G**ood-**B**ye **E**ddie.

Exercise 1: Naming the Strings

E – Eddie	A – Ate	D – Dynamite	G – Good	B – Bye	E – Eddie

THE MUSICAL ALPHABET AND BASIC INTERVALS

The musical alphabet only has seven letters: A, B, C, D, E, F, and G. Moving from one letter to the next is called a **step**. As you step through the alphabet, the notes get higher, and when you run out of letters, you start over at A. This eighth note is called the **octave** and has a very similar sound to the first note that was played.

Most of the notes are two frets from their neighbors, but some are only one fret apart. We say that a normal step, which is a distance of two frets, is called a **whole step**, while a **half step** consists of moving only one fret.

When stepping through the musical alphabet, we only encounter two half steps: from B to C and from E to F. Knowing this, we can name all of the notes on every string. Move two frets to get from note to note, except for B–C and E–F, where you'll move up just one fret.

Exercise 2: Notes on Each String

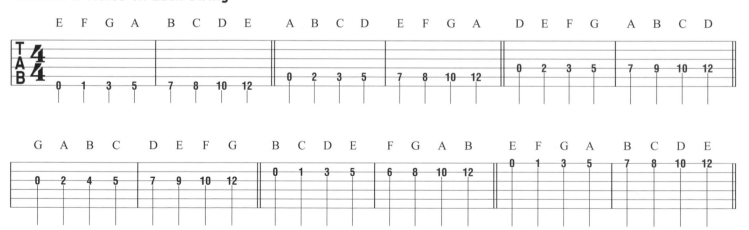

FRETBOARD ROADMAP

If you are trying to locate a note on a particular string, it can be time consuming and difficult to work your way up through a large number of notes. The 12th fret on the guitar is where you'll find the notes that are one octave higher than the open strings. Knowing that the 12th fret notes are E–A–D–G–B–E, you could start from there and step backwards through the alphabet to find a given note.

It is also useful to know the notes at the fifth and seventh frets. To learn the notes at the fifth fret, A–D–G–C–E–A, use this mnemonic device: **A**lways **D**o **G**uitar **C**hords **E**very **A**fternoon. To learn the notes at the seventh fret, B–E–A–D–F#–B, notice that the lower four strings spell the word "BEAD."

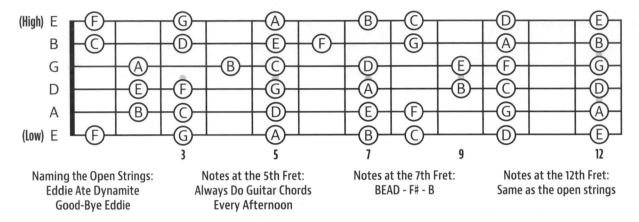

Exercise 3: Notes at the 5th Fret

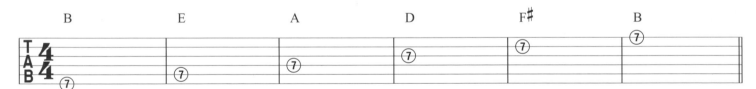

Exercise 4: Notes at the 7th Fret

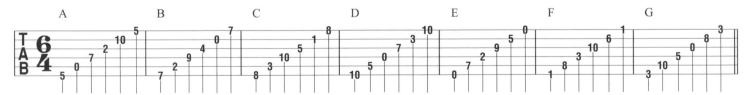

Exercise 5: Finding Notes on Every String

CHAPTER 3: MUTING

PALM MUTING

Palm muting is a technique that produces a slightly duller and more percussive version of a note. You achieve this sound by placing the side of your picking hand on the guitar strings, near the bridge, when you pick. You need to be right up against the saddle so you don't mute the strings too much and end up with a "clicky" or higher-pitched sound. You don't need to cover all six strings when you palm mute because you'll never play more than two or three strings at a time with this technique.

Exercise 1: Palm Muting

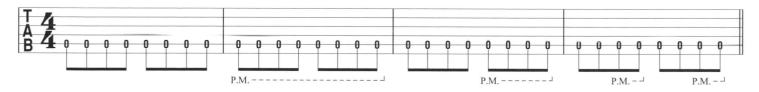

Exercise 2: Palm Muting

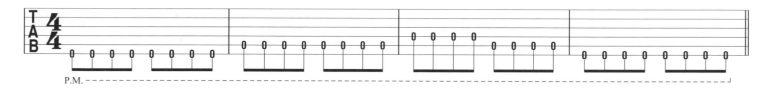

Exercise 3: Excerpt from Tchaikovsky's "Dance of the Sugar Plum Fairies"

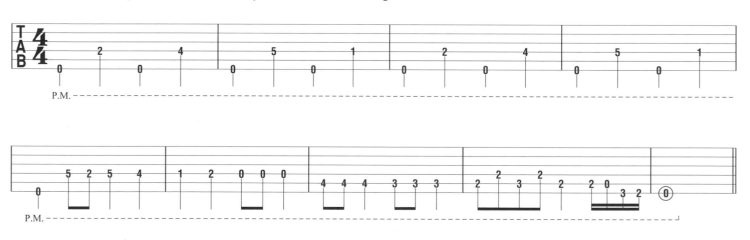

Exercise 4: Excerpt from Grieg's "In the Hall of the Mountain King"

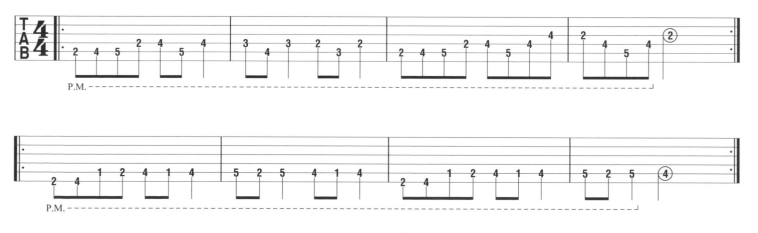

MUFFLED STRINGS

Muffled strings are strings that are strummed while simultaneously being muted by resting the fingers of your fretting hand on them. When you strum these strings, they will make a very percussive "clicking" sound. If you strum "down–up–down–up" while muffling the strings, you produce a "chucka-chucka" sound.

Exercise 5

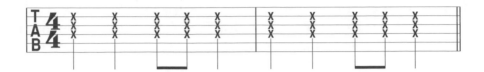

Exercise 6

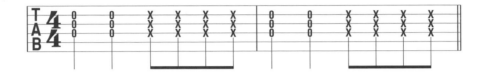

HANDLING BACKGROUND NOISE

Unwanted noise can be caused by strumming extraneous strings or simply by strings starting to sympathetically ring as a result of the guitar's vibration. To avoid these unwanted sounds, we often mute all of the strings that we're not intending to play. To quiet the unwanted strings, we use the same techniques that we use to execute palm muting and muffled strings. We prepare to palm mute unwanted low strings by laying our "free" fret-hand fingers across these strings and then strum the strings we actually want to hear. The clicking sound of strumming these muted strings is covered up by the notes we play. This way, we don't have to be too careful with our picking hand, all while keeping our guitar under control, even when using a very loud amp.

Exercise 7: Fret-Hand Muting—A Minor Pentatonic Scale

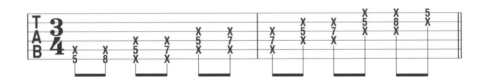

RAKING

You can use these muting techniques to accentuate a note, too. A **rake** is used to emphasize the sound created by strumming these muted strings. You can think of a rake as a slow strum across muted strings on your way to the intended note.

Exercise 8: Raking—A Minor Pentatonic Scale

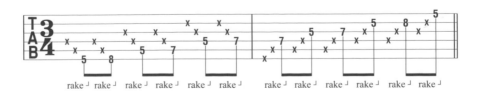

CHAPTER 4: STRUMMING

STEADY STRUMMING MOTION

Most of the strumming that guitarists use relies on a steady up-and-down movement of the strumming hand. The actual rhythm that you strum usually does not affect this up-and-down movement. It doesn't matter if you need to strum again right away or if you need to wait a moment before making another sound; keep your arm moving in time with the beat of the song—just move your hand in to touch the strings or out to avoid the strings as necessary. Don't stop your arm when you switch chords, either. Instead, start switching at the end of the previous measure so you can execute the new chord as you strum the first beat.

EIGHTH-NOTE STRUMMING

An **eighth note** is a note that lasts for one eighth of a measure in 4/4 time. You can also think of an eighth note as one half of a beat. For eighth notes in a measure of 4/4, we can count the downbeats and then say "and" on the upbeats: 1-and-2-and-3-and-4-and. There are eight counts total, so if we move our hand down on the numbered beats and up on the "ands," then we'll move eight times per measure.

Exercise 1

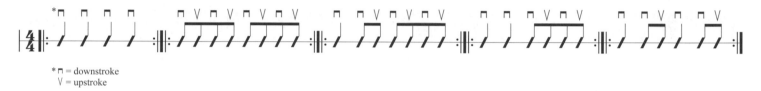

*⊓ = downstroke
V = upstroke

In 3/4 time, we do a similar motion but just count three beats before repeating: 1-and-2-and-3-and.

Exercise 2

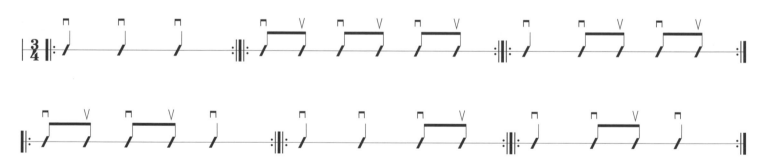

SYNCOPATION

Playing an accent that does not fall on the downbeat results in a kind of "skip" in the rhythm that is called **syncopation**. This can help our strumming patterns sound more interesting. A simple way to achieve this is to up-strum on two consecutive upbeats—without strumming the downbeat between them—like this pattern: down-down-up-skip-up-down-up.

Exercise 3

SWUNG EIGHTH NOTES

A different type of "skipping rhythm" can be achieved by making your downbeats twice as long as your upbeats. It's the normal sound of a quarter note followed by an eighth note in 12/8 time, but we often prefer the simplicity of counting in 4/4 time and just playing with a swing feel. The same eighth-note counting still applies, but now we pause a bit after the downbeats before saying "and" on the (shorter) upbeats. Think of the phrase "Hump-ty Dump-ty" when trying to play it.

Exercise 4

Exercise 5

16TH-NOTE STRUMMING

A **16th note** is a note that lasts for one 16th of a measure in 4/4 time. You can also think of a 16th note as one quarter of a beat. We add "e" and "a" to our eighth-note counting to come up with 16 counts: 1–e–and–a–2–e–and–a–3–e–and–a–4–e–and–a. You'll be moving your hand twice as fast now, and it will be even more common to strum and then just move past the strings without making contact to play longer notes while maintaining a smooth, steady motion.

Exercise 6

SECTION 2: CHORDS

This section gets into the nitty-gritty of playing chords. We'll build on what we've learned in Section 1: getting great tone, playing in time, and avoiding background noise when strumming.

What we'll learn in Section 2:

CHAPTER 5: POWER CHORDS

Open Power Chord Shapes, Movable Power Chord Shapes, and Movable Octave Shapes

CHAPTER 6: BASIC OPEN CHORDS

Major Chords, Minor Chords, and Power Chords

CHAPTER 7: I–IV–V PROGRESSIONS

Chord-Function Notation, and I–IV–V Progressions

CHAPTER 8: 12-BAR BLUES

The 12-Bar Blues Progression, the Quick Change, and the Turnaround

CHAPTER 9: CADENCES AND COMMON CHORD PROGRESSIONS

Cadences, the Doo-Wop Progression, the Pop Progression, and the Ballad Progression

CHAPTER 10: SEVENTH CHORDS

Dominant Seventh Chords, Major Seventh Chords, and Minor Seventh Chords

CHAPTER 11: BARRE CHORDS

Movable Chords, Sixth-String-Root (E-Shape) Barre Chords, and Fifth-String-Root (A-Shape) Barre Chords

VIDEO BANK ▶

Basic Open Chords

12-Bar Blues

Cadences and Common Chord Progressions

Seventh Chords

Barre Chords

CHAPTER 5: POWER CHORDS

Power chords are comprised of the first and fifth notes of the major scale. In sheet music and chord diagrams, power chords are referred to as "5th chords" (A5, E♭5, F#5, etc.). These two notes create a simple, clean harmony that sounds great with distortion and, unlike major or minor chords, doesn't conjure any happy or sad emotions.

OPEN POWER CHORD SHAPES

The shape of a simple, open power chord is easy to learn. Play an open E (low), A, or D string and pluck the next, higher string at the second fret. The open-string note is the root of the chord, and the fretted note is the 5th. You can also add the octave of the root note on the next, higher string. The only adjustment that must be made is on string 2, where the high D of the G5 chord is found at the third fret, while all of our other octave notes are found at the second fret.

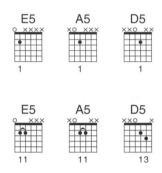

Exercise 1

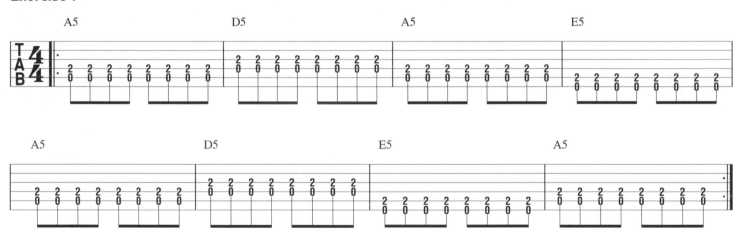

Exercise 2

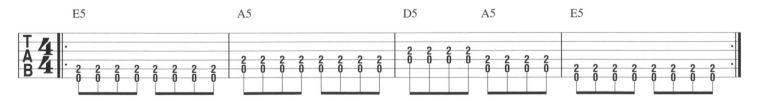

MOVABLE POWER CHORD SHAPES

It's not tough to play movable versions of these shapes. Play a note on the E (low), A, or D string and one on the next, higher string, two frets above the lower note. The lower-string note is the root of the chord, and the higher-string note is the 5th. Just like we did with the open shapes, you can also add the octave of the root note on the next, higher string. Also, just like before, when the highest note of a three-string power chord is on the B string, it's located three frets higher than the root note.

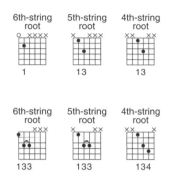

Exercise 3

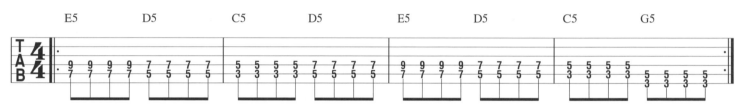

Exercise 4

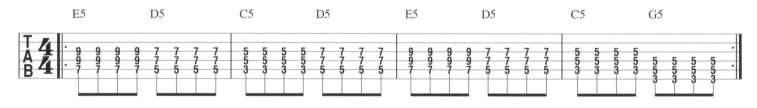

Exercise 5

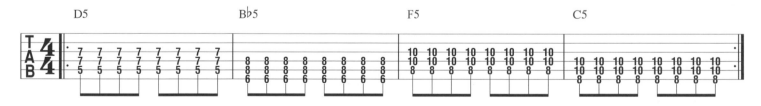

Exercise 6

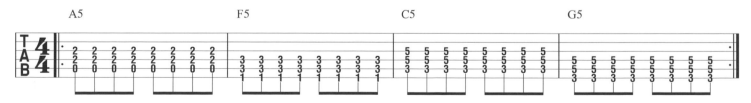

MOVABLE OCTAVE SHAPES

Another similar shape that we use often isn't even a chord; it's an octave. Since this shape is so similar to the three-string movable power chords, now is the time to learn it. Just mute the center string of the three-string power chord shapes, and you've got yourself a root note and an octave.

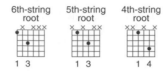

Exercise 7

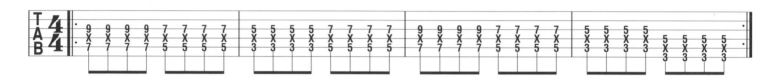

Exercise 8

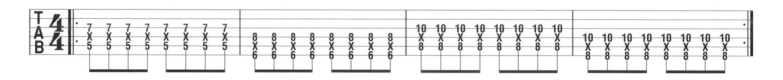

Exercise 9: "Twinkle, Twinkle, Little Star"

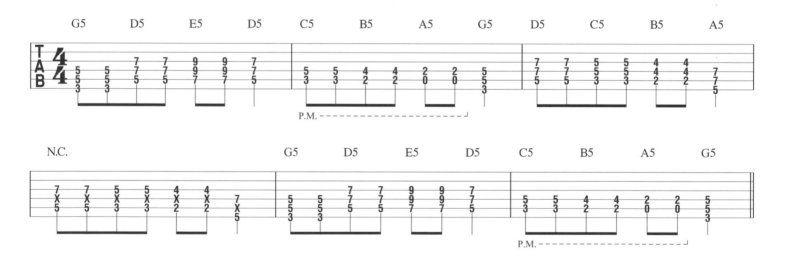

CHAPTER 6: BASIC OPEN CHORDS

Chords that include open strings are considered **open chords**. We'll include F in this category even though it doesn't have any open strings because it is a basic chord that is often played with other open chords. We'll cover some of the theory behind the chords as we learn them, but there are a few things to keep in mind: When you play any chord, you can have multiple instances of the same note, in different octaves. Also, pay attention to whether the strings you aren't fretting should be ringing or muted.

OPEN MAJOR CHORDS

Major chords are comprised of the first, third, and fifth notes of the major scale. In sheet music and chord diagrams, major-chord names are usually indicated by just the root note (A, E♭, F♯, etc.) rather than "A Major," for example. The relationship between the root and the third note of the major scale, which is referred to as the **major 3rd**, is happy sounding. It's this note that makes the chord a major chord. There are a few common ways to play A and G, so they've all been included.

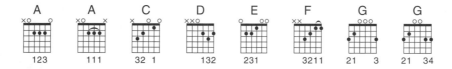

OPEN MINOR CHORDS

Minor chords are comprised of three notes, as well—in this case, the root and fifth notes of the major scale, and a minor 3rd. The minor 3rd is one half step lower than the major 3rd. In sheet music and chord diagrams, minor chords are usually denoted by the root note and a lowercase "m" (Am, E♭m, F♯m, etc.). The relationship between the root and minor 3rd is dark or sad sounding. It's this note that makes the chord a minor chord.

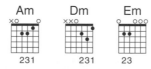

OPEN POWER CHORDS

We've previously learned that power chords are comprised of the root and fifth notes of the scale, so if we mute the 3rds from our major or minor chords, then we get some new, open power chord shapes. These chords sound great with distortion, and they don't have the happy or sad sounds associated with major and minor chords.

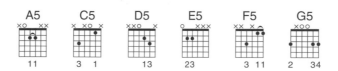

CHAPTER 7: I–IV–V PROGRESSIONS

CHORD FUNCTION NOTATION

If we say we are playing a song in a certain key, then we are going to mainly play notes from the major scale with the same root note as our key. If we look at each of the seven notes in the key and try to find a major or minor chord to play that only uses notes from our key, then we'll end up with the following pattern:

- The chords with root notes at the first, fourth, and fifth notes of the key are major chords.

- The chords with root notes at the second, third, and sixth notes of the key are minor chords.

- A major or minor chord played at the seventh note of the key doesn't line up with the notes in the key.

This pattern is the same for every key, so we sometimes use chord-function notation to explain the relationships between the chords in a progression, regardless of the key. Chord-function notation is simply a Roman numeral representing the position of the chord relative to the root of the scale, using uppercase letters for major chords and lowercase letters for minor chords. This practice is called the **diatonic pattern of chords**, or simply the **harmonized major scale**. Here is the diatonic pattern of chords written in chord-function notation:

The Diatonic Pattern of Chords:

I   ii   iii   IV   V   vi   vii°

The chord that lines up with the seventh note in the key is a **diminished chord**, so we've used a lowercase Roman numeral and the ° symbol for that one. Diminished chords are not very common, and they sound pretty "harsh," so we won't cover diminished chords any further in this book.

I–IV–V PROGRESSIONS

The I, IV, and V are the only chords in a harmonized major scale that have major qualities. Every note in the key can be found in these chords, so we can use these three major chords to play a happy sounding accompaniment to any melody comprised of notes from the scale.

There are many songs that primarily use the I, IV, and V chords, so it is important to become familiar with these chords in keys that feature their use.

Key	I Chord	IV Chord	V Chord
Key of C	C	F	G
Key of G	G	C	D
Key of D	D	G	A
Key of A	A	D	E

Exercise 1: Key of C

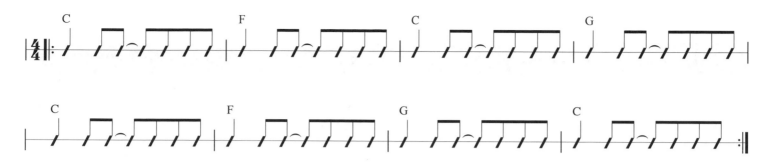

Exercise 2: Key of G

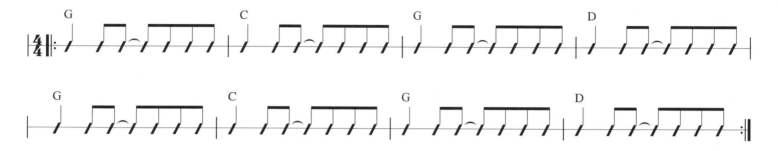

Exercise 3: Key of D

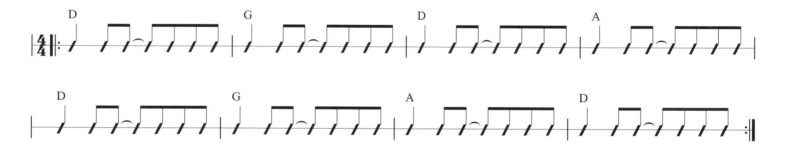

Exercise 4: Key of A

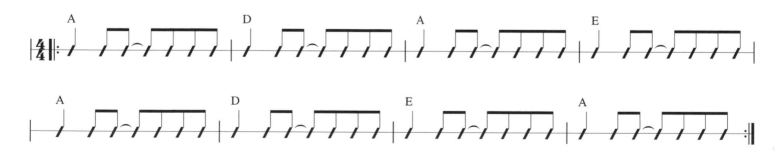

CHAPTER 8: 12-BAR BLUES

THE 12-BAR BLUES PROGRESSION

The **12-bar blues** progression is a type of I–IV–V progression that has been used in songs for the last century. The slow start with few chord changes, the busy ending with lots of chords, the 12-measure length, and the predictable sound are all contributing factors to its longevity and popularity. It also frequently features **seventh chords**, which we will cover in more depth in Chapter 10. Here's the basic pattern:

The 12-Bar Blues:

```
 |   |   |   |
IV  IV   |   |
 V  IV   |   V
```

Exercise 1: D Blues

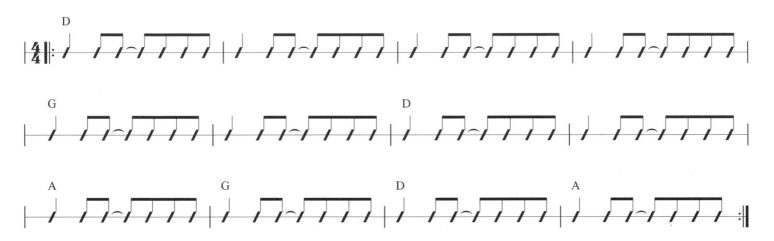

Exercise 2: A Blues

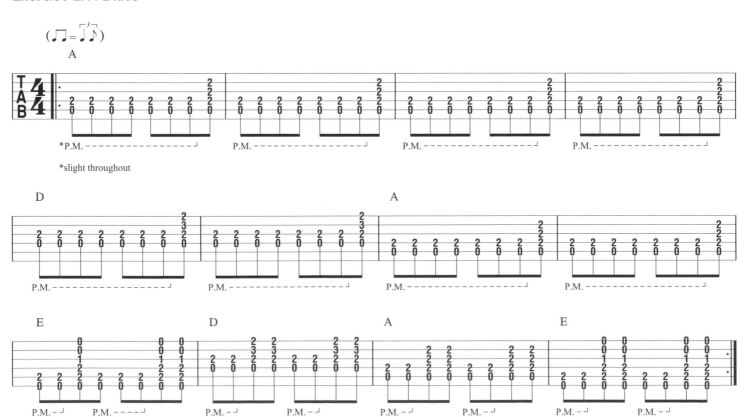

Exercise 3: E Blues

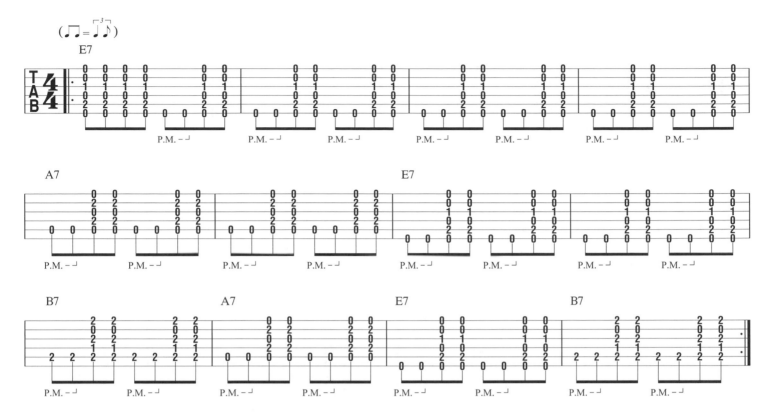

THE QUICK CHANGE

Here's a common variation, which features the **quick change** in the second bar:

12-Bar Blues with Quick Change:

```
I   IV  I   I
IV  IV  I   I
V   IV  I   V
```

Exercise 4: D Blues

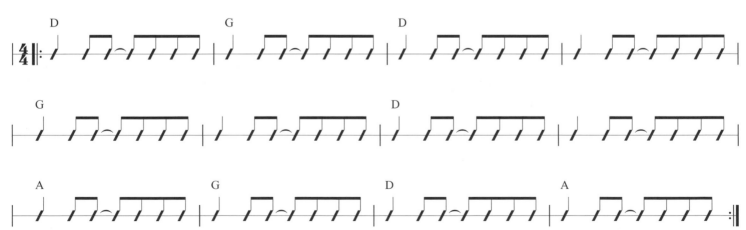

Exercise 5: E Blues

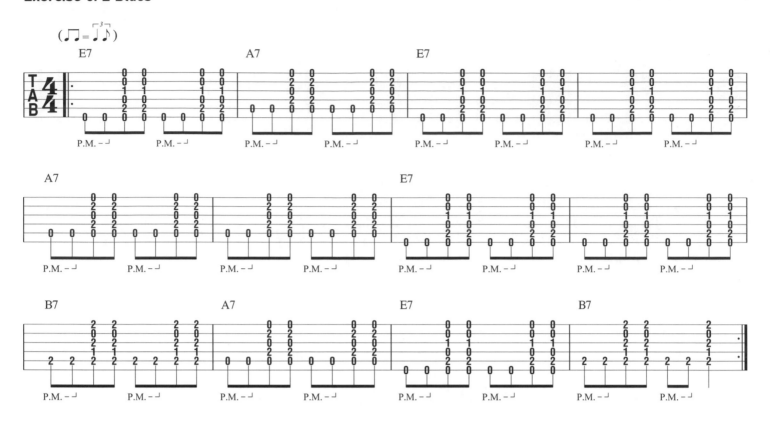

THE TURNAROUND

The last few measures are intended to signal a return to the beginning of the progression. This part of the 12-bar blues progression is called the **turnaround**.

Below is another common variation. It features the quick change and a different turnaround at the end:

12-Bar Blues with Quick Change and Alternate Turnaround:

```
 I   IV   I    I
IV   IV   I    I
 V  IV I IV I V
```

Exercise 6: D Blues

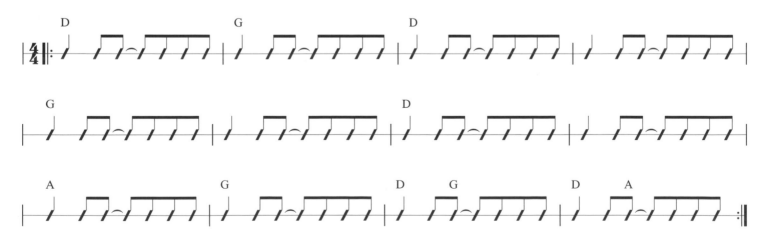

Exercise 7: E Blues Turnaround

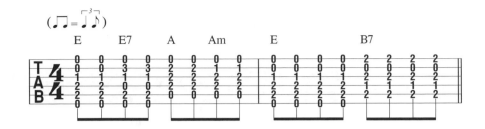

Exercise 8: E Blues

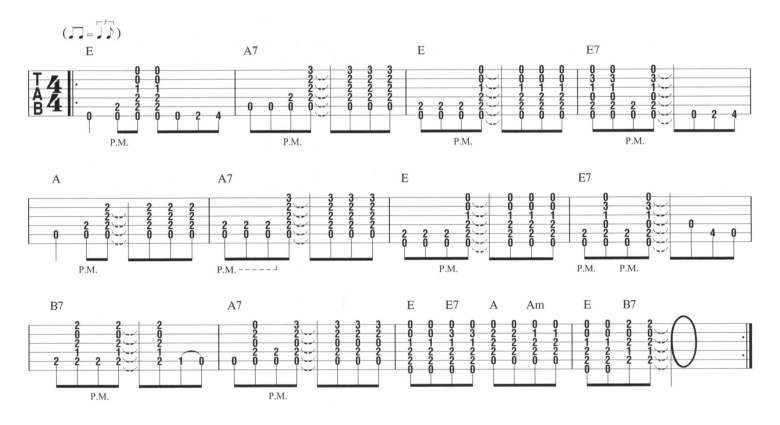

CHAPTER 9: CADENCES AND COMMON CHORD PROGRESSIONS

CADENCES

A **cadence** is a particularly strong sounding chord change that is usually used to signal the end of a phrase or section of music. Arriving at the destination chord in the cadence will produce either **tension**, an unfinished sound, or **resolution**, a finished sound. Using few cadences results in a softer or weaker sounding chord progression, while using many cadences results in a powerful sounding progression.

Type of Cadence	Initial Chord	Destination Chord	Sound
Authentic Cadence	V	I	Resolution
Half Cadence	Any	V	Tension
Plagal Cadence	IV	I	Resolution
Deceptive Cadence	V	Any (besides I)	Tension

With this in mind, take a look at the 12-bar blues, where you'll find a plagal cadence at measures 6–7. There's an unfinished-sounding half cadence in measures 8–9, a deceptive cadence in measures 9–10, and another plagal cadence in measures 10–11. In measure 12, we have a half cadence and, finally, an authentic cadence as we repeat the progression.

DOO-WOP PROGRESSION

After the I, IV, and V, the vi chord is the next most commonly used chord.

Here is a common progression popularized by the doo-wop music of the 1950s:

Doo-Wop Progression:

I   iv   IV   V

The IV–V change is a half cadence, and the V–I change that occurs as the progression repeats is an authentic cadence.

Exercise 1

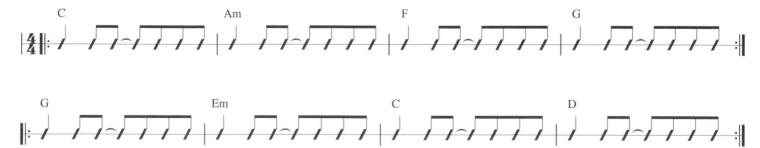

POP PROGRESSION

Here's another common progression that uses the vi chord found in rock and pop music:

Pop Progression:

I   IV   iv   V

The vi–V change is a half cadence, and the V–I change that occurs as the progression repeats is an authentic cadence.

Exercise 2

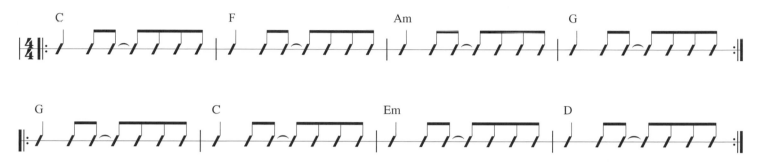

BALLAD PROGRESSION

Finally, we have another progression that uses the I, IV, V, and vi chords. This one is often found in slow songs or ballads:

Ballad Progression:

I   V   iv   IV

Many of the chord changes in this progression are cadences, so it sounds very powerful. The I–V is a half cadence, the V–vi is a deceptive cadence, and the IV–I at the repeat is a plagal cadence.

Exercise 3

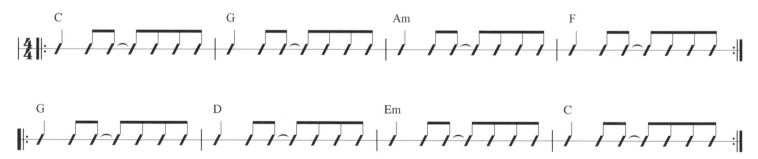

CHAPTER 10: SEVENTH CHORDS

Seventh chords, which we briefly introduced in Chapter 8, are chords that have a root, a 3rd, a 5th, and a 7th. Intervals of a 7th can be major or minor in much the same way as major and minor 3rds. If the 7th is the seventh note of the major scale, it is called a **major 7th**. If the 7th is one half step below the major 7th, it is called a **minor 7th**.

DOMINANT SEVENTH CHORDS

Chords with a root, major 3rd, 5th, and a minor 7th are called **dominant seventh chords**. They sound "unfinished" and are often used as the V chord in most keys, but they can be used in place of any chord for a bluesy or jazzy sound. Dominant seventh chords are usually just referred to as "seventh chords" and are notated with a "7" after the root note (A7, E♭7, F#7, etc.). Below are some common seventh chords, including popular alternate versions of A7 and E7.

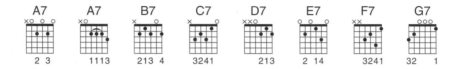

Exercise 1: E Blues

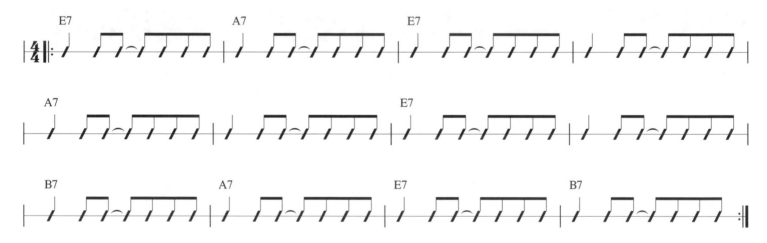

MAJOR SEVENTH CHORDS

Chords with a root, major 3rd, 5th, and a major 7th are called **major seventh chords**. They sound like sad versions of major chords and are used in the I and IV positions in the key. Major seventh chords are notated with "maj7" after the root note (Amaj7, E♭maj7, F#maj7, etc.).

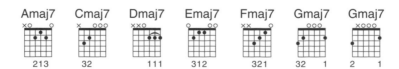

MINOR SEVENTH CHORDS

Chords with a root, minor 3rd, 5th, and a minor 7th are called **minor seventh chords**. They sound like happy versions of minor chords and are used in place of any minor chord. Minor seventh chords are notated with "m7" after the root note (Am7, E♭m7, F♯m7, etc.). Below are some common minor seventh chords, including popular, alternate versions of Am7 and Em7.

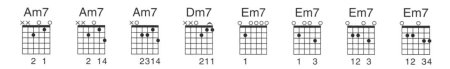

Exercise 2: Ballad

Exercise 3: Doo-Wop

CHAPTER 11: BARRE CHORDS

MOVABLE CHORDS

As long as we have enough fingers to hold down the spots that used to be open strings, we can create a movable chord from any open chord shape. We generally use our index finger to barre the strings that would have been open strings and then make the chord shape in front of the barre with our remaining fingers. Since this is difficult—or, in some cases, impossible—playing just a few strings from movable chord shapes is common practice, which we refer to as **partial chords**.

The most commonly used moveable chords are **barre chords** based on the E, Em, A, and Am shapes. The lowest note played by the index finger is the root of these chords. Using these movable major and minor shapes, we can play chords that don't have an open chord shape, like Bm.

SIXTH-STRING-ROOT (E-SHAPE) BARRE CHORDS

The movable, sixth-string-root chords use the first finger to barre all of the strings. These moveable chords are based on E, Em, E7, Emaj7, and Em7.

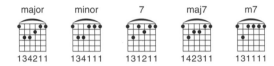

FIFTH-STRING-ROOT (A-SHAPE) BARRE CHORDS

The movable, fifth-string-root chords use the first finger to barre five of the strings much like the movable, sixth-string-root chord shapes. Notice that the movable, fifth-string-root major chord is a little different, however, as it uses the third finger to barre a few strings. These movable chords are based on A, Am, A7, Amaj7, and Am7.

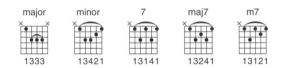

Exercise 1: Key of G

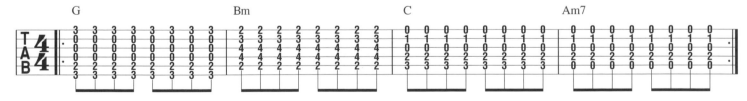

Exercise 2: Key of E

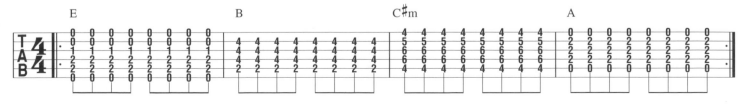

Exercise 3: Key of F

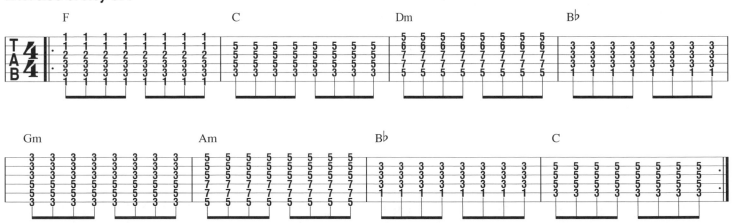

Exercise 4: Key of A

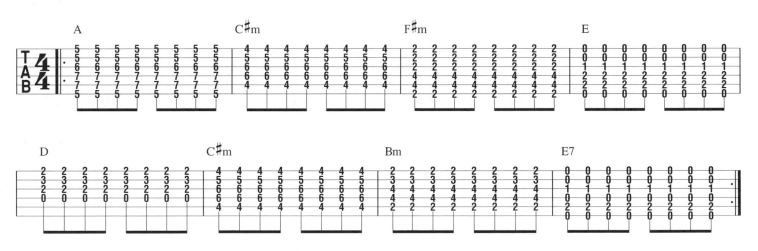

29

SECTION 3: ORNAMENTATION

We're switching gears now and looking into techniques that are used to add character and emphasis to single-note lines. This section will prepare you for playing lead guitar, using the scales that appear later in Section 4.

What we'll learn in Section 3:

CHAPTER 12: SLIDES

Sliding In and Out of Notes, Picked Slides, Legato and Grace-Note Slides, and Pick Scrapes

CHAPTER 13: HAMMER-ONS, PULL-OFFS, AND TRILLS

Hammer-Ons, Pull-Offs, Legato Phrasing, and Grace Notes

CHAPTER 14: BENDING

Quarter-Step Bends, Half- and Whole-Step Bends, Releasing a Bend, and Pre-Bends

CHAPTER 15: ADVANCED BENDING

Double-Stop Bends, Oblique Bends, Incidental Bends, Overbends, and Compound Bends

CHAPTER 16: VIBRATO

Consistent Cycles, Establishing the Target Pitch, and Vibrato Technique

CHAPTER 17: HARMONICS

The Harmonic Series, Natural Harmonics, and Pinch Harmonics

VIDEO BANK ▶

Slurs: Hammer-Ons, Pull-Offs, Trills, and Slides

CHAPTER 12: SLIDES

SLIDING IN AND OUT OF NOTES

We often slide up, into a note and down, out of a note to emphasize the beginning or ending of a phrase or to call attention to a particular pitch. It is also possible to slide down, into a note or up, out of a note, but these slides are far less common. The symbol for a slide into a note is a diagonal line before the note, and the symbol for a slide out of a note is a diagonal line after the note. As you move left to right, if the line goes up, then you should slide up, towards the bridge. If the line is going down, then you should slide down, towards the nut.

To slide into a note, start from just a fret or two away to help you arrive and stop at the right fret, and begin moving your finger a spilt-second before you pick the string. If you are sliding out of a note, then release the string pressure while you are sliding so the note never stops at any one fret, but instead trails off.

Exercise 1

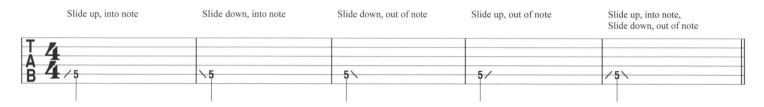

PICKED SLIDES

Sometimes we pick a note, then slide to another fret and pick that note. This is represented in musical notation by notes on both sides of a diagonal line. The angle of the line indicates whether this slide goes up or down, but there will only be one way to move from the first note to the second one.

LEGATO AND GRACE-NOTE SLIDES

Legato slides, also known as **slurred slides**, are slides that involve picking the first note and then sliding to the next note without picking the string again. These are notated with a diagonal line between two notes, like the picked slide, and a slur, which is a curved line connecting the two notes. If you make a sudden movement from the first note to the second one, you should be able to keep the string vibrating.

Sometimes these slides are supposed to happen extremely fast, immediately after the note is picked. This very fast first note is called a **grace note**, and it is notated with a note smaller than the regular-sized ones.

Exercise 2: Excerpt from Grieg's "Morning Mood"

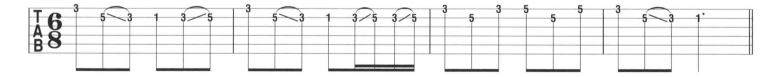

Exercise 3: Blues Riff

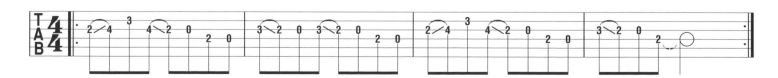

Exercise 4: Excerpt from Brahms' "Lullaby"

PICK SCRAPES

One special technique that produces a screeching sound is a pick scrape. Place the edge of the pick against the wound strings and scrape it against the strings. You may scrape for a while and then slide using your fretting hand to continue the sound while you get your pick back into playing position.

Exercise 5

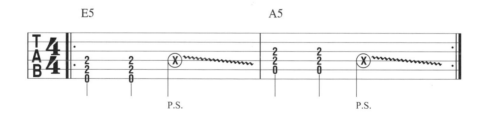

Exercise 6

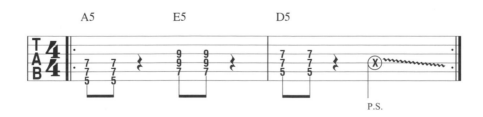

32

CHAPTER 13: HAMMER-ONS, PULL-OFFS, AND TRILLS

Slides aren't the only way to get from one note to another without picking. If you see a slur between notes but no diagonal line indicating a slide, then you'll either add a finger to a higher fret on the string or remove a finger to let a lower note sound.

HAMMER-ONS

A **hammer-on** involves adding a finger to a higher fret to make a higher pitch ring out without plucking the string again. The first note of a hammer-on can be an open string or a fretted note. Hammer-ons don't always happen immediately after picking the string, so pay attention to the rhythm of the notes. As the name implies, you'll need to pound down pretty hard so the string doesn't stop ringing when it touches your skin. The easiest way to get good tone with this technique is to be sure to press the string down right behind the fret, with a very sudden motion.

Exercise 1: Excerpt from Mozart's "Eine Kleine Nachtmusik"

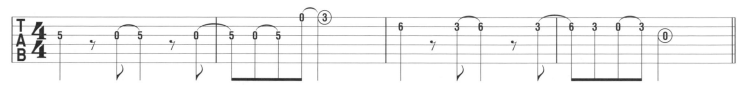

PULL-OFFS

The complementary technique, going from a higher note to a lower one without plucking the second note, is called a **pull-off**. The second note of a pull-off can be a fretted note or an open string. A pull-off is not as simple as just pulling your finger off of the string, however. You want the finger that you are removing to "pluck" the string as you pull off to ensure that the second note rings out.

Exercise 2: Excerpt from Mozart's "Eine Kleine Nachtmusik"

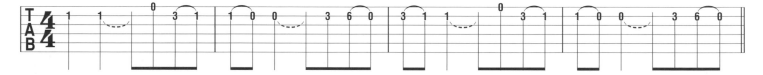

LEGATO PHRASING AND GRACE NOTES

We will sometimes see multiple notes connected with the same slur notation. Smoothly connecting several notes this way is called **legato phrasing**. It involves picking the first note of the slur and playing the rest of the notes with legato slides, hammer-ons, or pull-offs.

Exercise 3: Excerpt from Mozart's "Eine Kleine Nachtmusik"

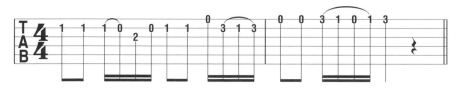

A very common example of legato phrasing is a **trill**, which involves repeatedly alternating two notes via hammer-ons and pull-offs.

Exercise 4: Excerpt from Mozart's Piano Sonata No. 16 in C major

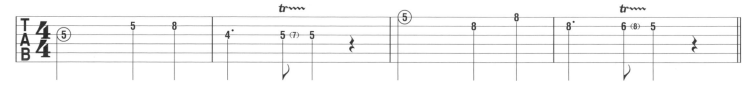

Just like with slides, we can perform these slur techniques so fast that you can barely discern the first note; these are called **grace notes**. Even though we are playing these notes very quickly, be sure to use proper technique.

Exercise 5: Excerpt from Mozart's "Eine Kleine Nachtmusik"

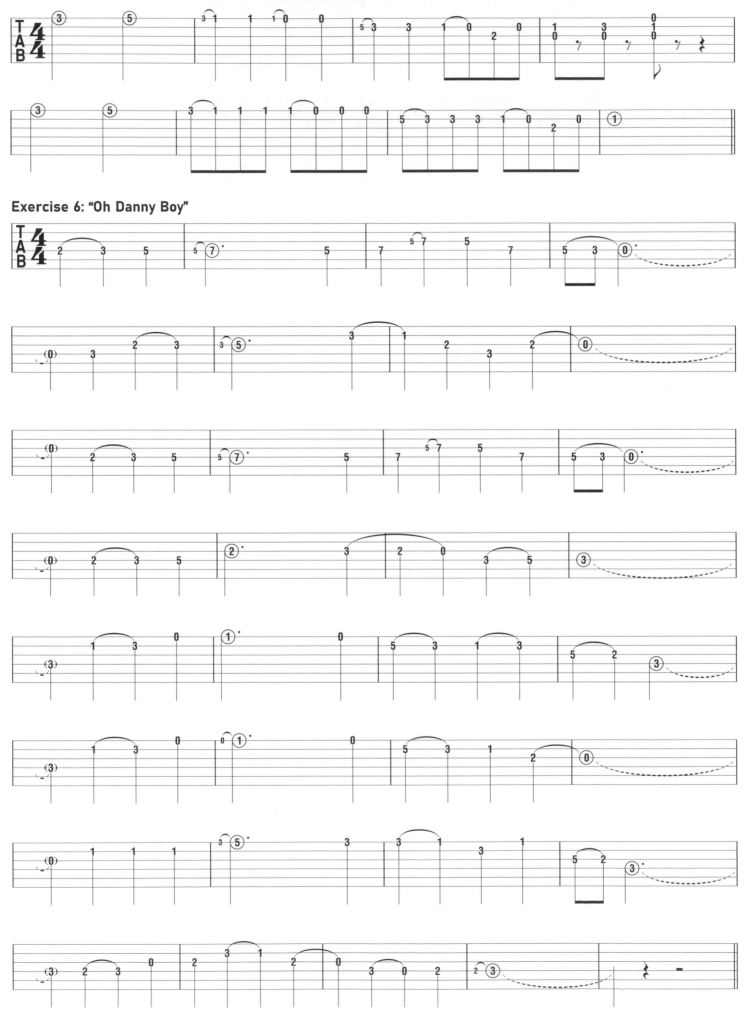

Exercise 6: "Oh Danny Boy"

CHAPTER 14: BENDING

Bending involves pulling or pushing a string towards other strings while fretting a note. This increases the tension of the string, which, in turn, raises the pitch. Cradle the neck of the guitar in your hand so you can use the thumb to get some leverage to bend the strings. We usually use our ring finger to bend the strings at the intended fret, with the middle finger also on that string to help pull or push. Since it's so short, we usually avoid using the pinky, but you can bend with any finger, really. Also, you can bend towards the ceiling or towards the floor, depending on which string you're bending and which string you're playing next. In the notation, you'll see a line moving up, which represents the pitch of the moving string, as well as an indication of how far the pitch should move, which is expressed in quarter, half, and/or whole steps.

Be sure to use the muting techniques we've learned to eliminate the background noise that can be caused by bumping into neighboring strings.

QUARTER-STEP BENDS

Quarter-step bends, also known as **blues bends**, are bends that keep changing pitch the entire time the note is ringing. This distance of a **quarter step** is the amount that we want to raise the pitch of the note. A quarter step is half the distance of a half step—in other words, as a bad-sounding, out-of-tune note that is higher than the current fret, but lower than the next fret. In order to make a pleasing sound when we play these bends, we raise the pitch in a slow, continuous motion for the full duration of the note. The listener hears the movement but never locks in on a specific pitch because the bend is always changing the pitch.

Exercise 1: Blues Lick

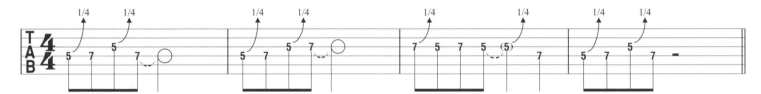

HALF- AND WHOLE-STEP BENDS

Half- and whole-step bends involve raising the pitch of the bent note by one or two frets, respectively. Once the note is in tune at the higher pitch, keep it there until you've purposefully stopped the string from vibrating.

Exercise 2: "Long, Long Ago"

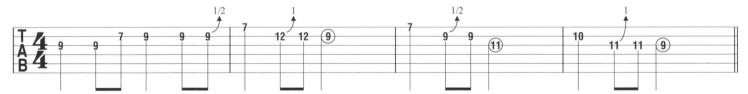

RELEASING A BEND

Releasing a bend means returning the string to its original, unbent pitch. Hold tight and make sure that you are squeezing the string against the fret (not the fretboard!) so you get a smooth change in pitch while keeping the string ringing. In the notation, a bend-and-release looks a bit like a shark fin as the line showing the pitch moves up and then down.

Exercise 3: "Long, Long Ago"

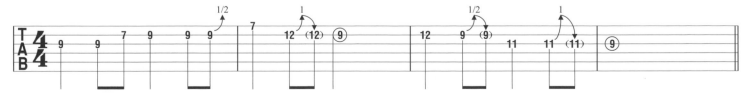

PRE-BENDS

A **pre-bend** is when you bend the string before you pluck it. In the notation, a pre-bend is indicated with a straight, vertical line to show that you hear the bent note, but you don't hear the pitch rising. Pre-bends are often paired with the release technique, and the combo is known as a **pre-bend and release**.

Exercise 4: "Long, Long Ago"

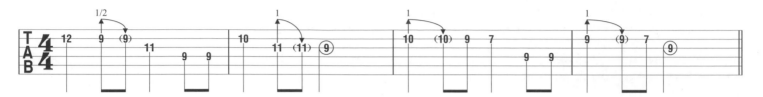

CHAPTER 15: ADVANCED BENDING

DOUBLE-STOP BENDS

Double stops are small, basic chords comprised of just two notes. Bending two strings at the same fret with a barre will result in an uneven but cool sound as the string held by your fingertip bends a little further than the other string. (See measure 5 of the exercise below.)

OBLIQUE BENDS

Oblique bends are bends in which one string is held while another note is bent, but both notes are allowed to ring out. Another name for these is "pedal-steel bends" since they can be used to mimic the sound of that instrument. When the note we are bending ends up at the same pitch as the note we are holding, we call it a **unison bend**. (These two types comprise most of the bends in the exercise below.)

COMPOUND BENDS

Compound bends are bends that happen in stages: We bend to a particular target pitch, and then bend higher to reach another target pitch. (See measure 27 of the exercise below.)

Exercise 1: "My Wild Irish Rose"

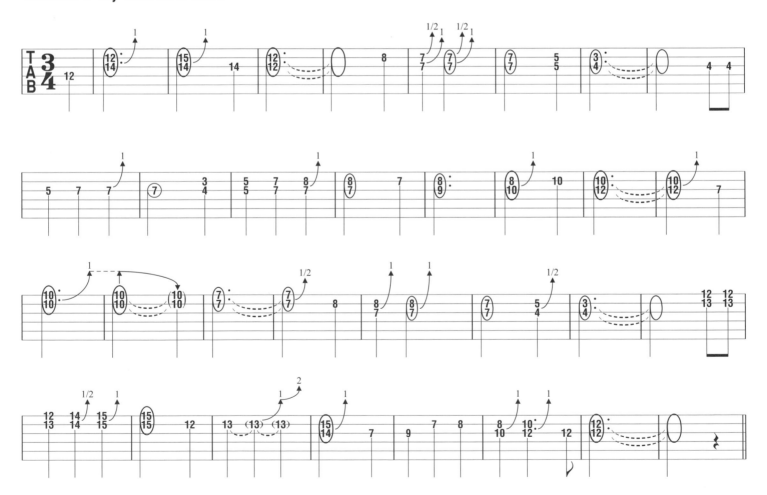

OTHER TYPES OF BENDS

Incidental Bends

An **incidental bend**—picking a neighboring string that is fretted by the finger that you are using to bend another note—can be an interesting bluesy sound, whether it is intentional or a "happy accident."

Overbends

Bending a string more than a whole step is known as an **overbend**. Overbends have a really great vocal quality and really catch the listener's attention since they aren't heard as often as half- and whole-step bends. Consciously place the tip of your finger on the side of the string opposite of the direction in which you are going to bend. This will keep the string from sliding underneath your finger when bending it so high.

CHAPTER 16: VIBRATO

Vibrato adds variety and depth to the sound of a note by repeatedly wavering from the target pitch and then reaffirming it. A long note that might sound stale without vibrato will benefit from the smooth change of being slightly out of tune and then back to the original pitch. We'll use a technique very similar to bending to accomplish this movement. The speed and the distance of the bend will vary, depending on the style of music or type of song, and the technique may vary, depending on the type of note being played. However, there are two important elements of vibrato that don't change: 1) the note needs to consistently move in and out of tune, and 2) you must establish the target pitch before starting the vibrato.

CONSISTENT CYCLES

If the speed of the vibrato is varied, then the listener will notice that change instead of focusing on the return to the original note. We notice how high and low a note goes as its pitch moves up and down, so it is very important to always go out of tune by the same amount and always return to the target pitch.

ESTABLISHING THE TARGET PITCH

The listener will notice the pitch of the note when it is first sounded. If you are already applying vibrato when you strike the string, then the first sound will not be the intended target pitch. This out-of-tune pitch will sound like the most important point of the vibrato, so the note will sound out of tune even if the rest of the technique is well-executed.

For "regular" notes, just pluck the string and wait a moment before applying vibrato. If you are applying vibrato to a bent note, then bend up to the target pitch, wait a moment, and then start cycling in and out of tune.

VIBRATO TECHNIQUE

For bent notes, you will use your forearm (not the knuckles of your fingers) to slightly release the bend before bending back up to original bent pitch. Your knuckles are for bends and your forearm is for vibrato.

Exercise 1: Vibrato with a Bent Note

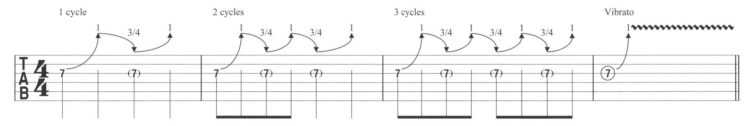

Unbent notes will be repeatedly bent and released. Again, try not to change the bend of your knuckles. Also, you won't bend up, then bend down, then up, then down, and so forth. Instead, the vibrato motion will always go in the same direction for the full duration of the note.

Exercise 2: Vibrato with an Unbent Note

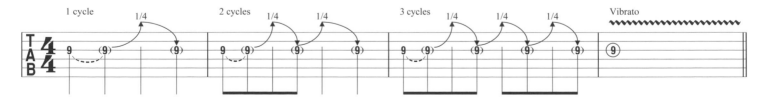

Execute the vibrato motion by rotating your forearm. Hold your fretting hand with the palm facing the bridge and the neck resting on the side of your hand near the index finger. Next, roll the hand along the neck to make your palm face the ceiling. This helps you notice how it feels to rotate the forearm and pivot where the side of the hand touches the neck, instead of at the fingertip.

Exercise 3: Excerpt from Beethoven's Symphony No. 5 in C minor

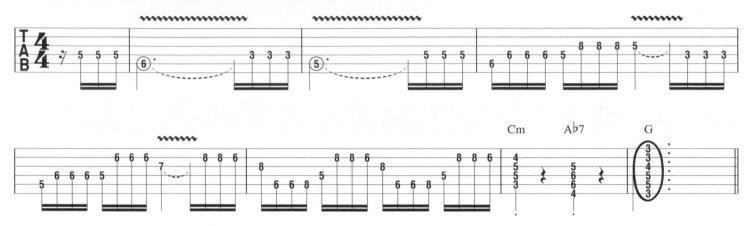

To develop a good feel for vibrato, you can execute the bend-and-release technique over and over again without bending at the knuckles.

CHAPTER 17: HARMONICS

The vibrations of the strings on your guitar are complex. If you pluck an open string, you hear a rich sound comprised of many vibrations. The full length of the string is wiggling back and forth, but there are also smaller waves that are making fractional portions of the string wobble back and forth in spite of the main vibration. When we isolate these vibrations that are happening at fractional lengths of the strings, we get **harmonics**.

THE HARMONIC SERIES

When you pluck a string in the normal place, a few inches from the bridge, the portion of the string that you pluck starts moving before the whole string can follow suit. The upper half of the string moves one way, sending the lower half in the other direction. Similarly, the upper third of the string moves in one direction, the middle third moves the opposite way, and the lowest third moves contrary to that. This continues for the fractional lengths of the string that make up what is known as the **harmonic series**: 1, 1/2, 1/3, 1/4, 1/5, 1/6, etc. Look up Newton's Laws of Motion if you want to get deeper into the physics; we'll concentrate on playing the guitar in this book!

NATURAL HARMONICS

The main vibration of the string, also known as the **fundamental frequency**, can be heard with fewer harmonics if you pluck it with your pick near the 12th fret. This prevents the fractional portions of the strings from moving in opposite directions. To isolate one of the other harmonics, we need to touch the string very lightly at the proper distance to split the string into a nice, fractional distance (halves, thirds, fourths, etc.) when we pluck it.

Place your finger on the string, directly above the 12th fret, to split it into two equal halves and then pluck it. Don't make the string contact the fret; just rest your finger on it. This will create a **node**, a point on the string where it is not vibrating, when you pluck it. The chime-like tone that you hear is the harmonic created by the string vibrating at half of the fundamental frequency.

Now try picking while resting your finger directly above the seventh or 19th frets. This will create a node that splits the string into three equal chunks.

The fifth fret is where you can split the string into fourths. The fourth, ninth, or 16th frets will split the string into five equal parts. There are even higher-sounding harmonics, but they can be tough to play when you are first learning this technique.

Exercise 1: Excerpt from Grieg's "Morning Mood"

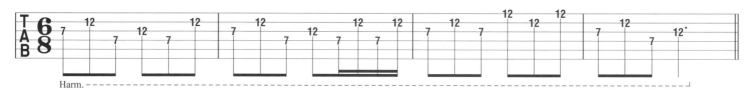

Exercise 2: Excerpt from Foster's "Oh, Susannah!"

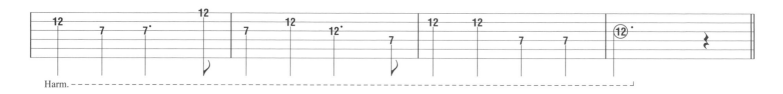

PINCH HARMONICS

You can actually use the thumb of your picking hand to create nodes by lightly bumping it into the string as you pluck a note. This lets you isolate the harmonics of any note, not just the pitches of the open strings. Though it is hard to get the notes above the 12th fret to produce natural harmonics, you can get a "squealy," higher-pitched version of any note by playing a **pinch harmonic**.

Exercise 3: "Three Blind Mice"

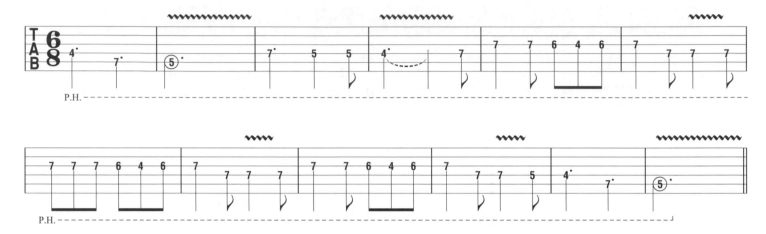

SECTION 4: SCALES AND IMPROVISATION

This section is intended as a reference to provide useful scale diagrams as you start to improvise some guitar solos. Some improvisation techniques are included to help get you started, as well.

CHAPTER 18: LEARNING SCALES

Learning Movable Scales, Sequenced and Contoured Scales, and Playing Efficiently

CHAPTER 19: IMPROVISING

Phrasing, Motivic Repetition, and Planning and Listening

CHAPTER 20: MINOR SCALES

The Minor Pentatonic Scale, the Minor Blues Scale, and the Minor Scale

CHAPTER 21: MAJOR SCALES

The Major Pentatonic Scale and the Major Scale

VIDEO BANK ▶

Learning Scales

Improvising

Minor Scales

Major Scales

CHAPTER 18: LEARNING SCALES

Improvising means making up the music you are playing as you go rather than playing a prepared piece. A good amount of lead guitar playing is improvised in almost every style of music. We learn scales as movable shapes so we can solo in any key by simply moving our scale patterns to different frets. Once you know that you are playing the pattern at the right fret, you can rely on the fact that every note in the scale will sound good as you solo.

LEARNING MOVABLE SCALES

As you learn these movable scales, the most important thing to do is learn where the root notes are located. In order to play in the right key, you need to play the pattern at whichever fret makes the root notes land on the desired root note of the song. Emphasize these notes as you learn the scale to reinforce the location of the root notes.

We usually learn scales in box patterns. That means we block out the frets above and below the area that our fingers can reach, playing only the notes within this box. To make the scales easier to remember and use, concentrate on learning one octave at a time. Learn these smaller one-octave patterns within the larger box pattern by only playing from one root note to the next. Then, play through the notes in reverse order to get back to the root note that you started on.

You'll notice that these one-octave patterns are found in the other box patterns of the scale; they'll just start on different strings. There may be slight changes in the shape, depending on where the B string is located within the octave pattern, but these similarities will help you learn the box patterns quickly.

SEQUENCED AND CONTOURED SCALES

Going through the scales in order is a good start, but you should also try to play patterns by starting at each note in the scale in order to develop some "muscle memory" of the scales. For example, choose a small number like 3 or 4 and play that many notes in a row, starting at the root note. Now, play that number of notes again, but this time starting at the second note of the scale, and then the third, fourth, and so on. This is called **sequencing a scale**. A complex pattern that repeats on each note is called a **motive**, and the resultant larger pattern is a **contoured scale**. Be sure to use both ascending and descending patterns when practicing this.

PLAYING EFFICIENTLY

Keep your index finger held down on a string as you fret higher notes with your middle, ring, or pinky fingers so you can move your hand as little as possible, as well as help your weaker ring and pinky fingers sufficiently fret notes. When moving to a different string at the same fret, with the same finger, be sure to roll from one string to the next. Also, don't forget to incorporate fret-hand muting so the picking hand doesn't have to aim perfectly to get the right sound.

CHAPTER 19: IMPROVISING

You get better at improvising by practicing improvising. It's OK to just noodle around in a scale, but it is best to play with some sort of a rhythm and chord structure. You can play along with drum tracks or full-band backing tracks, jam with friends, record yourself and then solo over the recording, or just solo over recordings of songs.

PHRASING

A short musical statement is a **phrase**. As you improvise, try to split your melody up into small chunks that relate to one another. Knowing where your notes fall in the beat is crucial when trying to play phrases that build upon one another.

Phrase repetition means playing the exact same phrase at the exact same place in the beat. It can be harder than it sounds, so make sure that you are able to do this. Once again, it's not just playing the same notes; you should be able to play them with the same rhythm, starting at the same count within the beat.

MOTIVIC REPETITION

One way to make your phrases sound like they belong together is to make a small change to the first phrase that creates the second phrase. This could mean playing the same notes with a different rhythm, playing the same rhythm with different notes, playing the same motive at a different spot in the scale, or some combination of these changes.

To practice **motivic repetition**, just make a small change to one note from your first phrase. An easy way to do this is to play a different note in place of the last note of the phrase. Another simple way to change a phrase is to play the last note sooner or later than you did in the initial phrase.

PLANNING AND LISTENING

You can make plans for how your phrases will be related to, or different from, one another. For instance, I could plan to play a high note, a four-note descending line, a three-note phrase, and then repeat the three-note phrase but make the last note the root note, so the solo will sound more like a well-thought piece of music and less like a random collection of notes.

Additionally, you should always be listening and reacting to what has been played. Perhaps you had a plan in place for a group of phrases, but after hearing what was just played, a new idea emerges. If you are bored, so is your listener. If you can't keep track of what you're doing, neither can your listener. If you are excited and intrigued by what you're hearing, you're doing it right!

CHAPTER 20: MINOR SCALES

MINOR PENTATONIC SCALE

We're starting with this scale because Pattern 1 of the **minor pentatonic scale** is the most often scale pattern used in blues and rock soloing. This scale sounds great over minor chords and progressions, but you can use it over many major progressions, as well.

Pattern 1	Pattern 2	Pattern 3	Pattern 4	Pattern 5

MINOR BLUES SCALE

The **minor blues scale** is constructed by adding one note to the minor pentatonic scale. The note we add is called a **diminished 5th**, and it has a very harsh sound. This "blue note" sounds very edgy, making this scale edgy sounding, as well. The minor blues scale is found in rock and metal, as well as in blues, jazz, and country music.

Pattern 1	Pattern 2	Pattern 3	Pattern 4	Pattern 5

MINOR SCALE

The **minor scale** can be very sad- or dark-sounding. It is used in many styles of music, particularly in sad songs, because of its moody quality.

Pattern 1	Pattern 2	Pattern 3	Pattern 4	Pattern 5

CHAPTER 21: MAJOR SCALES

THE MAJOR PENTATONIC SCALE

The **major pentatonic scale** is very happy sounding; there is barely any tension heard between the notes in this scale. The major pentatonic scale is often found in country and pop music.

Pattern 1   Pattern 2   Pattern 3   Pattern 4   Pattern 5

THE MAJOR SCALE

The **major scale** is what you are singing when you sing, "Do–Re–Mi." It is found in children's music because it has a very familiar and obvious sound, as well as in folk, country, pop, and pop-punk songs. Though it is associated with happy-sounding music, the major scale is often used in ballads, as well.

Pattern 1   Pattern 2   Pattern 3   Pattern 4   Pattern 5

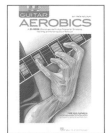

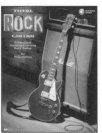